Contents

KU-652-230

Introduction

Wars are not only fought on the battlefield. They are also fought in the minds of the people doing the fighting – and those at home whose fate depends on the outcome.

Winning hearts and minds is the target of propaganda. The word *propaganda* comes from the name of a body set up by the Roman Catholic Church in the 17th century to spread the Catholic religion around the world. Today it is used to describe deliberate attempts to manipulate people's beliefs and actions. Sometimes propaganda makes a careful case using facts and arguments, but it can also be based on rumours, distorted versions of the truth or even on complete lies. Propaganda also often uses symbols, such as flags and insignia, architecture, music and particular words.

In wartime, there are two main types of propaganda. One, sometimes called white propaganda, aims to reassure the side that produces it. The other – black propaganda – aims to mislead or demoralize the enemy.

Forms of Propaganda

In World War II, propaganda was disseminated in a variety of ways. Governments carefully controlled what was reported in newspapers, for example, to make sure that it did not undermine people's morale. Poster campaigns had the same effect, as did patriotic films. Radio stations provided a way of directing propaganda at the enemy, by mixing political messages with entertainment, such as dance music. Aeroplanes dropped leaflets on occupied countries, either urging the occupied people not to give up hope or urging the occupying soldiers to go home. In Germany and Japan, governments used propaganda to indoctrinate their peoples with the belief that they were racially superior to the enemy. In Britain and the United States, politicians used more subtle – but still one-sided – campaigns to persuade their citizens how vital it was to resist the spread of fascism.

Effect of Propaganda

The combatants in the war ran the biggest propaganda campaigns of all time. It is impossible to judge how much they influenced the eventual outcome of the war. At the time, people believed that, without them, defeat was more likely, because they ensured that people kept fighting. In reality, many people did not fight for the ideas spread by propaganda but for more practical reasons – in order to defend their homes, families and friends.

This U.S. poster uses caricatures of Hitler to list and reject the arguments of German propaganda. The German message was that democracy was too weak to resist the Nazis' determination.

HITLER WANTS US TO BELIEVE THAT:

卐 Democracy is dying.

卐 Our armed forces are weak.

卐 The "New Order" is inevitable.

卐 Jews cause everybody's troubles, everywhere.

卐 We are lost in the Pacific.

卐 Our West Coast is in such grave danger there is no point in fighting on.

卐 The British are decadent, and "sold us a bill of goods."

卐 Some sort of "peace" can be made with Nazi Germany.

卐 The cost of the war will bankrupt the nation.

卐 Civilian sacrifices will be more than we can bear.

卐 Our leaders are incompetent; our Government incapable of waging war.

卐 Stalin is getting too strong, and Bolshevism will sweep over Europe.

卐 Aid to our allies must stop.

卐 This is a "white man's war"; our real peril is the Japanese, and we must join Germany to stamp out the "Yellow Peril."

卐 We must bring all our troops and weapons back to the United States, and defend only our own shores.

卐 The Chinese, the British, and the Russians will make separate peace with Japan and Germany.

卐 American democracy will be lost during the war: the two-party system is dead; Congressional elections will never again be held.

THE BRITISH BZ-Z-Z Z-Z-Z-Z-Z

THE AMERICANS BZ-Z-Z Z-Z-Z-Z-Z

AMERICANS WILL NOT BE FOOLED!

Allied Propaganda

⇑ **The King and Queen visit bombed-out areas in the East End of London.**

At the start of the war, Britain was the only major combatant that had evaded German control. But the British lived with a real fear of invasion or of being cut off and starved into defeat. It depended on its allies for supplies.

It became clear to the British government early in 1939 that German aggression in Europe might lead to war. The British set up a government department to produce propaganda aimed at Germany and the territory it had occupied. It also set up the Ministry of Information to produce 'white' propaganda aimed at encouraging British civilians. The ministry used various means of communication, including posters and radio broadcasts, which were organized by the young British Broadcasting Corporation (BBC).

Protecting the Country

The major focus of British propaganda was defence and security. It was feared, particularly early in the war, that the Germans could attack at any time. For that reason, everyone was encouraged to always carry their gas masks. There were drills at school and in workplaces, so that people knew how to fit their masks quickly.

⇒ **Buckingham Palace was bombed seven times during the war, but King George VI and Queen Elizabeth remained in residence.**

SPORTING FINAL
★★★★★
BID AND ASKED PRICES

The Sun

SPORTING FINAL
Sport Results on Page 35
7th EDITION

VOL. CVIII—NO. 10—DAILY.

NEW YORK, FRIDAY, SEPTEMBER 13, 1940.

THREE CENTS.

5 BOMBS HIT BUCKINGHAM, BUT MISS KING AND QUEEN

41 KNOWN DEAD AFTER JERSEY POWDER BLAST

WILLKIE WOULD SEND NO TROOPS TO WAR ABROAD

LONDON FASHION CENTER BOMBED BY NAZIS

MANY FEARED DEAD IN 3 LONDON RAIDS

ISSUED BY THE DIRECTOR OF PUBLIC INFORMATION UNDER AUTHORITY OF HON. J. T. THORSON, MINISTER OF NATIONAL WAR SERVICES, OTTAWA. PRINTED IN CANADA UE-41.

⇐ A Canadian beaver marches side by side with a British lion in this Canadian recruiting poster. The beaver has the maple leaf on its helmet; the lion's cigar is a reference to that of Winston Churchill (see box, page 10).

CHARLES DE GAULLE

When France surrendered to the Germans in June 1940 General Charles de Gaulle fled to London. He asked the British to let him broadcast messages to maintain morale in occupied France. He recruited a military force from French expatriates; troops and sailors from French colonies in Africa also joined. In 1942 de Gaulle also took charge of the resistance movement inside France.

⇒ **De Gaulle inspects Free French forces. By 1944, some 300,000 Free French took part in the D-Day invasion.**

⇒ **The 17th-century Canadian hero Pierre le Moyne was in some ways an odd choice for this recruiting poster: he had led a number of attacks against the British in Canada.**

In fact, a gas attack never happened. Instead, the bombing campaign known as the Blitz, which began in September 1940, meant that air raids on cities were common for around nine months.

Information

The Ministry of Information used posters to issue bulletins about the home front. These were simple lists of information, such as where it was possible to get hot meals, where people could volunteer to help at rest centres for bombed-out families and how people could get travel vouchers (nonessential travel was restricted). Local announcements included the term times for schools and colleges or the availability of new sites for bombed businesses. There were also more general tips on how to try to avoid sickness in crowded air-raid shelters, such as 'Gargle daily night

Eyewitness

HAROLD HOBDAY

Harold Hobday was a navigator on one of the Lancaster bombers that took part in the Dambusters Raid.

'I think it was a good thing, especially from a morale point of view. The dams raid, apart from anything else, did a lot for the morale of the country and abroad. It also did a lot of damage in Germany. So when people say "Was it worth it?" I say that it was.'

⬇ The *Daily Mirror* announces the success of the Dambusters Raid, which was later made into a famous film.

and morning' and 'Bring a handkerchief and always cough or sneeze in it'.

The threat of air raid remained throughout much of the war. Posters recruited members of the civil defence forces, such as air-raid wardens. They also gave the public a pictorial guide to help distinguish the shapes of enemy and friendly aircraft in the skies overhead.

Business as Usual

Despite the threat of bombardment or invasion, propaganda promoted an approach described as 'business as usual'. In difficult conditions, it was considered essential for morale to maintain the appearance of normal life as much as possible. Even today the British are often proud of their 'stiff upper lip', which means that they supposedly betray little emotion. One famous poster that summed up the British spirit remains popular. Its slogan reads simply, 'Keep Calm and Carry On'.

DAMBUSTERS RAID

Some military operations were as important for their impact on morale as for their actual results. One example was the RAF raid on the dams of the Ruhr Valley, one of Germany's vital industrial areas. The raid used a special bomb designed by Barnes Wallis. The bomb bounced along the water behind the dam, then sank and detonated next to the dam wall. The mission destroyed two of the four dams, but its real impact was to boost British morale. Wallis's ingenuity and the courage of mission leader Guy Gibson were widely celebrated.

Secret Campaign

The secret Political Warfare Executive was created in 1941 to aim propaganda at the Axis powers (Germany, Italy and, later, Japan) and at people living under occupation. It created radio stations to broadcast messages to enemy soldiers in Europe and organized the dropping of leaflets over occupied territory. The radio reported the steady Allied progress in the war, which German authorities did not tell their own people about. It was hoped that such messages would help to undermine German morale, but there was little evidence that such tactics worked.

Hello 'Auntie'

The British Broadcasting Corporation or BBC, then known as the Home Service, broadcast news and entertainment, as

WINSTON CHURCHILL

Churchill, who became British prime minister in 1940, was a controversial figure. In wartime, however, he was a figurehead. He was famous not just for his inspirational speeches but also for visual trademarks such as his cigar, hat and the V sign, made with his first two fingers. The gesture stood for victory.

⬇ Churchill was a remarkable speaker with a gift for inspiring quotes that were widely broadcast and reported in the newspapers.

BLACK-OUT 9.48 p.m. to 4.14 a.m.
Sun rises 4.44 a.m. sets 9.18 p.m.
Moon rises 7.38 p.m. sets 4.16 a.m.

DAILY SKETCH. TUESDAY, JUNE 18, 1940.

CALL-UP OF 3 CLASSES! PAGE

THE HOUSEWIVES HELP-MEAT- H·P SAUCE

Daily Sketch

No. 9,708 (E*) TUESDAY, JUNE 18, 1940 ONE PENNY

'I know what I like!'
Brown & Polson CUSTARD POWDER
BROWN & POLSON *Custard*

'We Shall Fight On, Unconquerable'

U.S. Hears Premier's Words

IN a short, historic broadcast last night, relayed to the United States, the Prime Minister, Mr.

BECOME THE SOLE CHAMPIONS, NOW IN ARMS, TO DEFEND THE WORLD CAUSE.

advance into France continued in full force.
● Mussolini accompanied by Count

well as coded messages to agents in occupied countries such as France. Even to own a radio in occupied territory was a serious crime. The call sign was the first four notes of Beethoven's Symphony No.5. Its rhythm was the Morse code, signal for 'v', or 'victory'.

'London calling' – the phrase that introduced the BBC news – was widely seen as marking the most reliable source of information on the course of the war, even when fighting spread into distant regions of the British empire, such as

⇓ **This poster shows a British soldier and a French worker as comrades in order to stress that French resistance to the Germans continued in the shape of the Free French led by Charles de Gaulle.**

BRITISH ASIA

There were many subjects of the British Empire who believed that World War II had little to do with them. Some Indians and Burmese saw the British as their colonial oppressors. They were more hopeful that a British defeat might lead to independence. The British tried to convince them that Japanese rule would be worse than being in the empire. The Japanese, meanwhile, used propaganda to encourage Asians who were unhappy to take up arms against the British forces.

UN SEUL COMBAT POUR UNE SEULE PATRIE

Burma and India. Many observers believe that the reputation the BBC enjoys today as a source of global news was created during World War II.

Other innovations used entertainment to boost morale. They included the creation of the music-dominated Light Programme, now Radio 3. Some of the shows that began during the war are still broadcast today, such as *Woman's Hour* and *Book at Bedtime*.

The Commonwealth

When Britain declared war on Germany, the members of the Commonwealth did the same. In Australia and Canada, in particular, propaganda encouraged volunteers to enlist for military service. In India, however, some Indians were reluctant to fight for the British. They wanted independence – which they finally received in 1948.

German Propaganda

Adolf Hitler was a firm believer in the power of propaganda to influence people's behaviour. Long before he came to power he explained his beliefs in the book *Mein Kampf*.

Hitler argued that, at the end of World War I, Germans had been convinced by Allied propaganda to abandon support of the German army, which then had to surrender. This argument, which was very popular in Germany in the 1920s, was completely false. The German army had surrendered in 1918 because its military defeat had become inevitable.

Big and Small Lies

The fact that Hitler's central argument was based on a falsehood reveals something about how he viewed propaganda. He thought that it did not matter whether or not it was true.

MEIN KAMPF

Hitler wrote *Mein Kampf* ('My Struggle') when he was in prison in 1924. It laid out most of his beliefs, including hatred of the Jews and a willingness to lie in order to get and retain political power.

OLYMPICS

In 1936 Berlin staged the Olympics. The Nazis saw it as a chance to prove the superiority of the German race. In fact, the star of the games was African American Jesse Owens, who won four gold medals. In the long jump, he beat Nazi poster boy Lutz Lang. Hitler refused to award the gold medal to Owens, instead leaving the stadium.

⟹ The Olympics were a showcase of German efficiency and modernity.

Ein Volk, ein Reich, ein Führer!

⇑ Although Adolf Hitler was a civilian, posters portrayed him wearing militaristic clothes, as befitted a war leader.

JOSEPH GOEBBELS

As head of propaganda Goebbels staged events like an exhibition of 'degenerate' art – particularly by Jews – and the burning of 'un-German' books. Later he promoted 'total war' to involve the public in the war. Before Hitler killed himself, he named Goebbels as his replacement. But the next day Goebbels poisoned his children, then he and his wife killed themselves.

⬇ **This poster, issued by Goebbels in 1944, stresses that Germany will never capitulate to the Allies.**

ALLES
kann in diesem Kriege
möglich sein,
NUR
NICHT,
daß wir jemals
KAPITULIEREN

DR. GOEBBELS

In fact, Hitler argued, people were more likely to believe big lies than small ones. He wrote: 'In the primitive simplicity of their minds they more readily fall victim to the big lie than the small lie, since they themselves often tell small lies in little matters but would be ashamed to resort to large-scale falsehoods.' In other words, if a lie is big enough, no-one will ever believe that it could have been made up.

Propaganda

Hitler argued that people could be persuaded to adopt almost any views. But he had fixed ideas about how propaganda should work. It had to be simple and direct, because most people were not very intelligent or receptive to new ideas. 'All effective propaganda must be limited to a very few points and must harp on these in slogans until the last member of the public understands what you want him to understand by this slogan.'

> **"** *It is the absolute right of the state to supervise the formation of public opinion.*
> **JOSEPH GOEBBELS** **"**

Eyewitness

LENI RIEFENSTAHL

Riefenstahl filmed the 1934 Nazi Party Congress in Nuremberg. Her film was a propaganda classic, *Triumph of the Will*.

'[Hitler] wanted a film showing the rally through a nonexpert eye, selecting just what was most artistically satisfying – in terms of spectacle, I suppose you might say. He wanted a film which would move, appeal to, impress an audience which was not necessarily interested in politics.'

Propaganda Supremo

When Hitler and the Nazis took power in 1933, Hitler had the chance to put his theory into practice. The man in charge was his ally Joseph Goebbels, minister for propaganda. Goebbels had been in charge of Nazi propaganda since 1926. He had run a campaign to increase the party's popularity and had developed Nazi symbols such as the swastika (a broken cross), the eagle and the wreath of laurel leaves. He staged huge rallies with masses of Nazis carrying banners. Goebbels presented Hitler as a soldier (even though he wore civilian clothes).

⇐ A 1944 issue of an Austrian magazine boosts German morale with a photo of the V-1 flying bomb being used to attack Britain.

NAZI RALLIES

Among the events organized by Goebbels was a series of Nazi rallies. Goebbels had a great sense of the theatrical and lined up thousands of Nazis with swastika banners. Everything was intended to show the power of the state over the individual. At Nuremberg, architect Albert Speer created a dramatic arena for the yearly party congress, which took place at night with dramatic lighting.

⇐ Nazi troops parade with swastika banners during a rally at Nuremberg.

Goebbels showed Hitler standing up for a country that had been treacherously defeated in a just conflict.

In 1939 Goebbels produced a poster that featured a portrait of Hitler with the slogan, 'One people, one empire, one

⇑ **Adolf Hitler (right) and other Nazi leaders examine a painting at an exhibition of 'degenerate' art organized by Joseph Goebbels.**

leader'. The poster was so popular that in many homes, offices and classrooms it replaced religious pictures and crucifixes.

Goebbels' Targets

Goebbels' Ministry of Propaganda concentrated on two major aspects of Nazi ideology. First it argued that Germany needed to expand in order to

MASTER RACE
One key Nazi belief was that the Germans belonged to a Nordic race called the Aryans. The blonde, blue-eyed Aryans were more racially pure than other peoples. The Nazis believed that made them a superior race.

survive: all Germanic peoples should be brought into an empire that would cover much of central and eastern Europe. Second it set out to convince the German people that they were the *Herrenvolk*, or master race. In particular, the Nazis blamed Germany's economic problems on the Jews, who were portrayed as being subhuman (later in the war, Slavic peoples were treated in a similar way). Jews were even shown as having animal features. In contrast, Nazi posters idealized Germans, who were portrayed as handsome, blonde, blue-eyed and physically fit.

ANTI-SEMITISM

When Hitler blamed Jews for Germany's suffering after World War I, he was echoing a long history of anti-Jewish feeling (anti-Semitism) in Germany and central Europe. The Nazis wanted to persuade Germans that Jews were an inferior race so that they could carry out their plan to segregate and exterminate them. Posters depicted Jews as ugly bankers, taking money from honest people. As the war went on, the depiction of Jews became less human. In one film, Goebbels showed them as rats living in the sewers: he wanted to suggest that Jews were a race of vermin.

National Socialism

In the early months of the war, Germany won rapid victories in Poland, France and the Low Countries with its tactic of *blitzkrieg* or 'lightning war'. It was easy for Goebbels to maintain the fiction of German superiority. Every week his office produced a new poster to hang in all party offices, military barracks and public buildings. The posters carried simple quotations with no illustration. The slogans included 'National Socialism is the guarantee of victory', 'The Führer

⇓ **This Nazi poster claims that the Allied powers are in fact being run by a secret Jewish conspiracy.**

Hinter den Feindmächten: der Jude

> **During a war, news should be given out for instruction rather than for information.**
> **JOSEPH GOEBBELS**

is always right' or 'No-one can get past the German soldier'.

In May 1941, when the last quotation appeared, the opinion it expressed seemed to be true. The German Army had conquered western Europe, Poland, the Balkans and Greece. In June 1941 Germany invaded the Soviet Union. Again, it won many initial victories. It also began an extermination campaign against Jews, communists and others. Propaganda began to warn of the threat from the Bolsheviks – Russia's communist rulers – who were again portrayed as being inhuman.

FEAR OF BOLSHEVISM

Hitler's invasion of the Soviet Union in June 1941 reflected his deep fear of communism. After early German advances, the Russians pushed the invaders back and began to march towards Germany itself. Goebbels' propaganda campaign highlighted the Bolsheviks as a threat to the whole German way of life. After the Nazi defeat at Stalingrad, Goebbels announced 'For the time being, propaganda against the Western powers will be secondary to propaganda against Bolshevism. In conjunction with our anti-Bolshevist arguments, these opponents, Churchill and Roosevelt above all, are to be presented as accomplices and toadies of Bolshevism. Bolshevism is the main enemy we have to fight against, which is the most radical expression of the Jewish drive for world domination.'

The tone of the propaganda grew more desperate after the defeat of a whole German army at Stalingrad in January 1943. The Sixth Army had besieged the city for months but had in turn been encircled by Soviet forces. Its surrender was a huge blow to Nazi morale.

Total War

Although Nazi propaganda often resorted to lies, even Goebbels could no longer maintain the fiction that the Germans were naturally superior to their enemies. Now German propaganda concentrated on the threat to Europe from communist Bolsheviks. Goebbels declared that the conflict was a total war. German women were sent to work in factories and offices

⇒ **Germans attend a 1937 anti-Semitic exhibition entitled The Eternal Jew.**

⇑ This poster of a German soldier and a Nazi 'Brownshirt' (stormtrooper) was painted by Mjölnir, Hitler's favourite artist.

for the first time. Goebbels announced, 'Now, people, rise up and let the storm break loose!' Posters showed grim-faced soldiers ready to defend the homeland. If the communists overran Germany, Hitler said, 'Man's efforts, stretching back over several thousand years, to create a civilization would have been in vain.'

As Germany's enemies advanced from both sides in 1945, such propaganda grew less effective. No-one could deny any longer the social collapse that they saw all around them.

⇒ This newspaper puts the defeat at Stalingrad in the best-possible light: 'They died so that Germany could live on.'

U.S. Propaganda

For most Americans, the war was taking place far away. U.S. propaganda concentrated on reminding Americans why the war was necessary. It also played an important role in maintaining national morale.

The United States had ended World War I in 1918 as the world's most powerful nation, militarily and economically. But the losses of nearly 120,000 men in Europe had upset Americans, who immediately after the end of the conflict had turned their backs on any international affairs that might drag them into another war.

From Prosperity to Depression

This practice, 'isolationism', meant that the United States did not join the League of Nations. This international body was set up by U.S. president Woodrow Wilson to resolve disputes peacefully.

↑ This rare photograph shows President Franklin D. Roosevelt being helped out of a car before a public meeting.

⇒ **The America First Committee was founded to keep the United States out of what its members saw as a European war. Soon after Japan attacked Pearl Harbor, it dissolved itself.**

```
ISOLATIONISM

Traditional U.S. foreign
policy was based on
isolationism. This was
the idea that the United
States was so wealthy, and
so isolated, that it could
remain separate from world
affairs. In fact, that was
rarely possible for such a
major superpower.
```

WAR'S FIRST CASUALTY

AMERICA FIRST COMMITTEE

141 West Jackson Boulevard
CHICAGO

⇒ **Norman Rockwell's famous 'Four Freedoms' posters pictured an idealised – and very popular – version of American life.**

The U.S. Congress refused to join the league, even though it was the president's own creation.

The 1920s was a period of financial success for the United States. At the end of the decade, however, the country was plunged into the Great Depression as trade slowed to a near halt. The world's richest nation had to get used to the sight of thousands of people sleeping rough or standing in line for food at soup kitchens.

The government of Franklin D. Roosevelt, elected in 1932, launched a programme of measures known as the New Deal to overcome the worst effects of the Depression. However, despite the New Deal, the U.S. economy had never fully recovered. By the time World War II began in 1939, Americans were still suffering from the economic crisis.

OURS...to fight for

Freedom of Speech

Freedom of Worship

Freedom from Want

Freedom from Fear

NORMAN ROCKWELL

Although he painted few official posters, Norman Rockwell was probably the most popular U.S. artist of the war. Best known for his covers for the Saturday Evening Post, Rockwell drew his subjects with great detail and elements of humour. The small-town America he portrayed was friendly, quirky and nostalgic; it was a place of plenty and harmony where everyone got along. Rockwell painted four posters illustrating the 'four freedoms' Roosevelt outlined as America's war aims: Freedom of Speech, Freedom of Worship, Freedom from Want and Freedom from Fear.

Disaster at Pearl Harbor

The humiliating circumstances of the attack on Pearl Harbor in December 1941 were another blow to U.S. confidence. It was only by chance that some of the fleet aircraft carriers were out at sea on exercises, or U.S. naval power in the Pacific Ocean might have been destroyed before the conflict even began.

Although there had been some signs that the Japanese were growing increasingly hostile towards the United States, it seemed that the U.S. forces were completely unprepared to defend themselves. Further bad news came with the defeat of America's colony in the Philippines early in 1942.

Resistance to War

Many Americans had been reluctant to go to war. Some thought that the Great Depression had showed that the United States should concentrate on solving its

⇓ **This crude anti-Japanese cartoon shows a worried Japanese admiral with a servant inviting him to commit hari-kiri, or ritual suicide.**

own problems. It did not need to get involved with quarrels between countries in Europe, on the other side of the Atlantic Ocean. That view was shared by those who believed in America's traditional isolationism. There were also millions of German Americans who did not want to go to war against Germany and a far smaller number of Americans who actually agreed with Nazi ideas.

Organizations such as the America First Committee (AFC) believed that Europeans should sort out their own disagreements. With 800,000 members at its peak, the AFC was set up in late 1940 to keep America out of the war. It argued that the United States should not supply war goods to the British, for fear of getting dragged into the conflict.

AN AFRICAN AMERICAN HERO

Doris 'Dorie' Miller was a cook on board USS West Virginia at Pearl Harbor on 7 December 1941, when Japanese aircraft attacked. African Americans were not allowed to take front-line jobs, so Miller was serving as a cook. When the attack began, he rushed up on deck under heavy fire and helped carry the injured captain to safety. He fired a machine gun at enemy aircraft until the attack ended. Miller's bravery won him the Navy Cross. He became a celebrated hero, partly because he reinforced an image of all Americans pulling together.

⬇ **This recruiting poster shows Dorie Miller wearing his Navy Cross. Miller was killed in action in the Pacific in 1943.**

Its supporters felt that Roosevelt had been planning to join the war since it began in September 1939. They were probably right. Roosevelt had favoured the Allies and supplied them with equipment. He used his regular radio broadcasts to try to convince Americans that the country should become the 'arsenal of democracy'. A poster campaign told workers that their war production was essential for the Allies to maintain democratic values in the face of the European dictators.

Changed Situation

Things changed with the attack on Pearl Harbor in December 1941. The United States was now at war with Japan; a few days later Japan's ally Germany also chose to declare war on the United States. The AFC voted to disband itself. Most of Roosevelt's critics now rallied behind the country.

One of the main purposes of U.S. propaganda was to make sure that Americans remained united in supporting the war effort. It also set out to boost national morale and confidence despite the disastrous start to the war.

V FOR VICTORY
The V symbol used on U.S. stamps was used in Allied countries to stand for 'victory'. It actually originated in Belgium in the early days of the war.

> *Remember Pearl Harbor –*
> *Keep 'em dying!*
>
> MOTTO OF U.S. ADMIRAL WILLIAM HALSEY

The Office of War Information (OWI) was created in 1942 to organize U.S. propaganda. As in other countries, the OWI set out to use any means it could to spread its message. The Bureau of Motion Pictures was established to get Hollywood studios to make films that portrayed a positive image of the country and the conflict. Newspapers cooperated by agreeing not to publish photographs that showed dead soldiers, for example. Radio stations broadcast to servicemen in Europe and the Pacific: they concentrated on a positive view of the war and on uplifting music. Even postage stamps were used to carry patriotic designs and messages. They included a famous V for 'victory' shaped by the wings of a stylised American eagle.

⇑ **Workers crowd the offices of the Office for War Information in Washington, D.C.**

OWI

After the humiliating defeat at Pearl Harbor it was important to maintain national morale. In June 1942 Roosevelt created the Office of War Information (OWI). Its purpose was to educate Americans about the dangers of fascism. It also promoted the image overseas of Roosevelt as the leader of the free world.

Poster Campaign

One of the OWI's main means of spreading information was through posters that appeared in post offices, schools, railway stations, restaurants and shops. During the Great Depression of the 1930s the government had begun to use artists to produce public artworks.

⇒ Even postage stamps were used to spread propaganda messages to help maintain U.S. morale.

The artists created posters or murals in public buildings. Now the OWI recruited outstanding commercial artists such as Norman Rockwell (see box, page 22) to produce a series of war posters.

It used a network of volunteers to distribute and display the posters it created. Members of volunteer defence councils took the 'poster pledge'. They agreed to treat posters 'as real war ammunition'. They would 'make every one count to the fullest extent' and 'never let a poster lie idle'.

Who Is the Enemy?

The early campaign concentrated on the nature of the enemy. There was already an undercurrent of distrust of East Asians among some Americans, based on immigration from Asia in the 19th and early 20th centuries. People saw these new arrivals as a threat to traditional U.S. society. Discrimination against East Asians was common. The early arrivals were mainly Chinese labourers who helped to build the transcontinental railways. Japanese immigration began in the late 19th century, mainly to Hawaii and later to the West Coast of California. At the time of Pearl Harbor, there were around 230,000 Japanese in the United States. Most of them were detained in internment camps.

Once the war began, newspapers were quick to condemn the Japanese as "the yellow peril". Posters showed them as dehumanized animals. U.S. newspapers were quick to report atrocities committed by Japanese soldiers. There were a number of incidents where Japanese troops treated native populations or U.S.

HOLLYWOOD

The Bureau of Motion Pictures was responsible for getting Hollywood to make morale-boosting films. The films showed the United States as a society united behind the war effort; or they showed America's fighting forces overcoming an evil enemy. In the three years of its existence, the OWI made changes to more than 500 films to fit with official policy.

⇒ **Humphrey Bogart and Ingrid Bergman star in** *Casablanca*, **one of the most famous films of the war.**

prisoners very harshly. On Bataan in the Philippines, for example, the Japanese forced 75,000 U.S. and Filipino prisoners of war to march about 100 kilometres (60 miles) on their way into captivity. Some 10,000 prisoners died from starvation or were murdered by Japanese soldiers when they became ill or too weak to march any further. After the war, the so-called Bataan Death March was condemned as a war crime. During the war, it was another way to whip up American hatred towards the Japanese.

Call to Arms

Posters also sounded a call to arms. 'Remember Pearl Harbor' was a powerful message. It stressed that the United States was the victim of unprovoked aggression that forced it to fight. U.S. propaganda argued that the conflict was a 'just war' because it countered Japan's imperialist conquests in Asia. That argument ignored the fact that the United States was itself the prewar occupying force in the Philippines (America had inherited the islands as part of its victory in the Spanish-American War of 1898). The war against the Nazis in Europe was also presented as a struggle to liberate oppressed people crushed by a militaristic conqueror. For the Americans – a deeply religious people, led by a deeply religious president – it was reassuring to have such reminders of the morality behind their war effort.

Soviet Propaganda

POSTER ART

Many Russians could not read. Few had radios. So posters were the most important means of mass communication. Artists had developed 'soviet' styles of illustration. The style was modern, with hard edges and flat colours. It was stylized and abstract rather than realistic. The lettering was often large and simplified, with short slogans. The posters were clear and direct, rather than subtle.

The Soviet Union was very different from the other Allies. Since 1923 it had been governed along strict lines by the communist dictator Joseph Stalin.

The communists had come to power in Russia after a revolution in 1917 led by Vladimir Lenin and his allies, the Bolsheviks. Under Lenin and his successor, Stalin, the Communist Party had come to control all aspects of life. In 1922 the old Russian empire was replaced by the Union of Soviet Socialist Republics, which included Russia and large parts of eastern Europe and Central Asia.

Changing the Soviet Union

Stalin's rule had become increasingly strict. In an effort to get farmers to produce more food he had forced them to join together in collectives. This policy, called collectivization, had failed badly.

⇩ Stalin (right), Roosevelt (centre) and Churchill meet at Yalta in the Crimea in February 1945 to discuss the aftermath of the war.

Пролетарии всех стран, соединяйтесь!

Всесоюзная Коммунистическая Партия (больш.).

ПРАВДА

Орган Центрального Комитета и МК ВКП(б).

№ 38 (9809) | Вторник, 13 февраля 1945 г. | ЦЕНА 20 КОП.

«Нашей непреклонной целью является уничтожение германского милитаризма и нацизма и создание гарантии в том, что Германия никогда больше не будет в состоянии нарушить мир всего мира».

(Из заявления руководителей трёх союзных держав о результатах работы Крымской Конференции).

Конференция руководителей трёх союзных держав— Советского Союза, Соединённых Штатов Америки и Великобритании в Крыму

Конференция руководителей трёх союзных держав — СССР, США и Великобритании в Крыму. На снимке: г-н У. Черчилль, г-н Ф. Д. Рузвельт, тов. И. В. Сталин.

Фото С. Гурарий.

I

Разгром Германии

V

Декларация об освобождённой Европе

SOVIETS

Government was organized through a series of committees known as 'soviets'. These committees were set up in workplaces and in military units.

⇨ 'Forwards to the West' announces this Soviet poster from 1942. At the time, the slogan was rather optimistic: the Red Army was actually still on the defensive.

ВПЕРЕД! НА ЗАПАД!

Продублировано издательством «Плакат»

Первое издание осуществлено Государственным издательством «Искусство» в 1942 г.

17

It contributed to a famine in Ukraine in the early 1930s that killed between 2.5 million and 10 million people.

In industry, meanwhile, Stalin set production targets for factories and for workers in a series of five-year-plans. These plans led to the modernization of Soviet industry. By the start of the war, the Soviet Union was one of the most industrialized countries in the world. Its

> " In the Soviet army it takes more courage to retreat than to advance. "
>
> **JOSEPH STALIN**

factories were churning out large numbers of tanks, artillery pieces and other modern weapons of war.

Old Heroes

One theme of Soviet propaganda was an appeal to Russia's past. This was unusual, because the communists valued loyalty to the Communist Party over loyalty to the old nation of Russia. Now, with the blessing of Stalin, propaganda appealed to the memory of Russian heroes. They included Alexander Nevsky, the medieval prince who defended Russia against foreign attacks; Mikhail Kutuzov, who defeated Napoleon's assault on Moscow in 1812; and Alexander Suvurov, who in the late 18th century had fought the Turks

ВОИНУ-ПОБЕДИТЕЛЮ-
ВСЕНАРОДНАЯ ЛЮБОВЬ!

⇐ **By 1944 Soviet posters reflected a more optimistic view: it was clear that Germany would be defeated on the Eastern Front.**

⇐ **Soviet troops distribute newspapers from Moscow in Poland at the start of the war, before the German invasion.**

and Poles. Cultural icons used to inspire patriotism included Leo Tolstoy, the great novelist, and Peter the Great.

Great Patriotic War

Stalin was a pragmatist. He knew that an appeal to Russian patriotism would be more effective than appealing to loyalty to the Communist Party. He also allowed the Russian Orthodox Church to reopen many of its churches for worship, even though the Soviet Union was officially an atheist state. Posters stopped using communist symbols, such as the hammer and sickle. Stalin set out to convince Russians to support the Great Patriotic War – the name he gave it, and by which it is still known in Russia today.

MOTHER RUSSIA

Two strong and related images in Russian propaganda were Mother Russia and the Motherland. They drew on centuries of Russian association with the land and traditional folklore. Mother Russia was an imposing babushka, or nurselike figure, who was responsible for protecting and looking after the land. Most Russians had a soft spot for such a babushka from their childhood. The German invasion, meanwhile, was a very real threat to the Motherland. Posters appealed to Russians' love of the Motherland rather than to loyalty to the communists. After the war a number of statues of Mother Russia were erected to celebrate the Soviet victory.

Japanese Propaganda

Japanese society had become more militaristic since the early 1930s. The military dominated the government. Its values were based on a code known as bushido, 'the way of the warrior'. These values were embodied in the traditional Japanese warrior, the samurai.

Japanese society, like the Japanese military, was based on ideas of honour and self-discipline. Such principles formed the basis of the education system. Even before the war began, propaganda stressed the 'purity' of the Japanese compared to their enemies.

Leaders of Asia

The other main purpose of propaganda was to convince Asian peoples that the Japanese could free them from rule by European colonial powers. The image of being liberators had a strong appeal among the Japanese, but was less popular among other Asians.

⇒ This poster proclaiming the 'Rise of Asia' shows the Japanese as the saviours of their neighbours, breaking the chains of Western imperial rule.

EMPIRE

Western powers had large colonies in Asia before the war. They included the British in India and Singapore, the Americans in the Philippines, the French in Indo-China and the Dutch in Indonesia. The Japanese presented their conquests as a campaign to free Asians from foreign rule. In fact, the 'coprosperity sphere' the Japanese wanted to create simply represented another form of oppression.

⇓ Military commanders meet Emperor Hirohito. The army pledged complete obedience to the emperor but in fact he had little power to prevent Japan's relentless approach to war.

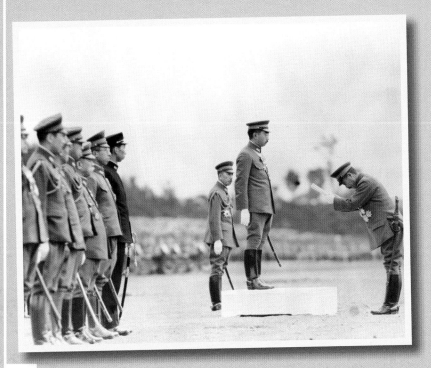

SAMURAI

Japan's military values were based on renowned medieval warriors named samurai. The samurai had a code of honour that included choosing death before surrender.

They were suspicious of Japanese control. In many cases they did not see much advantage in swapping Western rule for domination by a closer-at-hand Asian nation.

The Japanese accused western colonists who lived in Asia of stealing local wealth. Japanese soldiers were taught that 'Money squeezed from the blood of Asians maintains these small white minorities in their luxurious mode of life.'

An Asian Family

In 1942, the Japanese government published a booklet explaining that Asian countries would be like a family – with Japan as the father. The booklet promised that 'We will make the countries of Greater East Asia friendly to one another. We of Greater East Asia will combine our power and bring about the destruction of America, England and others.'

In reality, the Japanese were harsh rulers. When Japanese troops invaded China in 1937 – they had occupied the Manchuria region in 1931 – war broke out. The Japanese claimed to want stability for all Asians. But their soldiers committed atrocities against hundreds of thousands of Chinese, including using them for bayonet practice.

Superior Race

One motivation for Japanese behaviour was the belief that other Asian races were inferior. The Chinese in particular were

TOKYO ROSE

Many soldiers serving overseas listened to the radio, so all sides used broadcasts to try to convince enemy troops to turn against the war. In the Pacific the most famous propaganda presenter was Tokyo Rose. Rose was not one individual: U.S. forces used the name for anyone who broadcast Japanese propaganda from Tokyo. The woman most often associated with the name was Iva Toguri, who broadcast under the name Orphan Anne. Toguri was an American who was detained in Japan at the start of the war and forced to broadcast Japanese propaganda; in fact, she was careful never to say anything negative about the United States.

⇑ **Iva Toguri is questioned by American reporters at the end of the war; she later won recognition as an outstanding U.S. citizen.**

 This poster, 'Accepting an Allied Surrender', had special meaning for the Japanese. They believed that to surrender was a disgrace that reflected weakness and immorality.

portrayed as being subhuman, as the Nazis portrayed the Jews. Propaganda constantly reminded the Japanese of their spiritual purity and of the values that they embodied. These values included complete obedience to the emperor and a dedication to honour and respect.

Fatal Pride

Many Japanese resented their treatment after World War I. Although Japan had sided with the Allies, the United States and Britain limited the size of the Japanese fleet after the war to ensure that their own ships would dominate the Pacific. The Japanese also disliked depending on the outside world for imports (the United States, for example, supplied 60 per cent of Japanese oil).

Such dependence offended Japanese pride and intensified their resentment of the West. They saw Western countries as weak and cowardly, corrupted by luxury living. In contrast, the Japanese were self-disciplined and loyal; their code of honour meant that they would prevail. It

THE DIVINE EMPEROR

The Japanese worshipped their emperors as gods. They believed that the imperial family had descended from the sun goddess Amaterasu. Emperor Hirohito was Japan's figurehead, although the country was run by the military. It later turned out that Hirohito had been reluctant to go to war. After the war, the Americans forced Hirohito to tell his subjects that he was not divine. His radio announcement of the surrender was the first time most Japanese had ever heard his voice.

 The war has developed not necessarily to Japan's advantage.

EMPEROR HIROHITO

also meant that Japanese were reluctant to surrender, which they saw as a mark of dishonour. That was one reason why so many Japanese soldiers fought to the death and why hundreds of thousands of civilians preferred to commit suicide rather than fall into enemy hands.

Other Countries

It was not only the major powers who used propaganda in World War II. All the countries involved in the conflict sought to bolster the morale of their own citizens or undermine that of the enemy.

One country in which propaganda was highly advanced was Italy. The fascist dictator Benito Mussolini had come to power in 1922. As a former journalist, Mussolini understood the power of the media to persuade the public of one view or another.

Fascist State

The fascist state Mussolini created was supported by newspapers, radio stations, films and even school lessons that promoted his role as the saviour of Italy. The government closely controlled the media through the Ministry of Popular Culture. Mussolini ordered that his own name should always be written in capital letters when it appeared on posters. He also forbade newspapers from printing photographs of him dancing or in the company of priests. Instead, posters showed him stripped to the waist, working with peasants in the fields as a 'man of the people'.

Mussolini promised to lead Italy back to the greatness of the ancient Roman empire. Fascist symbolism echoed Roman designs.

⬆ 'The British treat all nations equally' declares this Italian poster. The bodies on the gallows are those of peoples who wanted freedom from British rule.

MACARTHUR'S RETURN

U.S. General Douglas MacArthur left the Philippines in 1942, when it became clear that the Japanese would conquer the islands. He promised 'I will return' and for the rest of the war, he pushed U.S. military planners to liberate the Philippines. His eventual return was a propaganda triumph. MacArthur was photographed wading ashore. The message was clear: no matter how long it took, the United States was loyal to its allies.

➡ MacArthur, in sunglasses, wades ashore on his return to the Philippines in 1944; he declared 'I have returned'.

The Office of Special Services in the United States produced this poster to boost resistance to the Japanese in the Philippines.

> **"** *Cinema is the strongest weapon.* **"**
> BENITO MUSSOLINI

Fascist architects designed buildings in the style of ancient structures. Mussolini sought swift military victories to bolster his empire. The Italians easily defeated Abyssinia (Ethiopia) in 1936 and Albania in 1939.

Real War

When the war began in 1939, however, Mussolini's boasts soon proved meaningless. The Italian army was badly prepared and had poor weapons. By the end of 1940 Italian forces were retreating in North Africa and an invasion of Greece had been halted and reversed. Two years later the Italians were driven from North Africa and the Allies invaded Italy itself.

In September 1943 the Italians surrendered to the Allies; Mussolini was killed by Italian fighters in April 1945.

PER IL NUOVO ORDINE SOCIALE, PER LA CIVILTÀ

⇑ This Italian poster shows soldiers from the Axis allies: Italy, Japan and Germany. It declares 'Conquer! For the New World Order!'

Eyewitness

BENITO MUSSOLINI

The Italian dictator Mussolini visited Adolf Hitler in Germany in 1938 during talks about the German occupation of Czechoslovakia. The previous year Hitler had persuaded Mussolini to become Germany's ally.

'Our welcome in Munich was fantastic and the Führer was very nice. Hitler is a sentimentalist deep down. When he saw me he had tears in this eyes. He really loves me.'

France

In France, meanwhile, the northern and western part of the country was under German occupation. The rest of the country, known as Vichy France, was in theory an independent nation but in practice a puppet state of the Germans.

Vichy propaganda aimed to convince the public that France's natural ally was

VICHY FRANCE

In June 1940 the Germans occupied much of France. The southeast remained nominally independent, under President Henri Pétain and Prime Minister Pierre Laval. This state, known as Vichy France after the town where its government was based, was controversial. Some of its governors agreed with Nazi ideas; others wanted to maintain a French state, even if it was not fully independent. But Vichy did cooperate with the Nazis, for example by deporting French Jews to concentration camps.

⇐ **Henri Pétain (right) and Admiral Jean Darlan, chief of the Vichy France navy, leave a French war memorial in January 1941.**

Germany rather than Britain. Its rallying cry was the sinking of French vessels by the British in North Africa at the start of the war, to prevent them falling into the hands of the Germans when the French surrendered. Some 1,700 French sailors died in the attack, which seriously damaged relations with Britain even among the majority of French people who were opposed to Germany.

Like the Nazis, the Vichy regime blamed a Jewish conspiracy for starting the war. It presented the war as a struggle to save France from communism, which it said was the real duty of patriots. Such propaganda was contradicted by broadcasts from London by General De Gaulle. He argued that France needed to free itself from German control.

⇒ **This Vichy poster of a drowning sailor urges French citizens not to forget British attacks on French naval vessels at Oran, Algeria, soon after the fall of France in 1940.**

N'oubliez pas Oran!

Timeline of World War II

1939

SEPTEMBER:
German troops invade and overrun Poland
Britain and France declare war on Germany
The Soviet Union invades eastern Poland and extends control to the Baltic states
The Battle of the Atlantic begins
NOVEMBER:
The Soviet Union launches a winter offensive against Finland

1940

APRIL:
Germany invades Denmark and Norway
Allied troops land in Norway
MAY:
Germany invades Luxembourg, the Netherlands, Belgium and France
Allied troops are evacuated at Dunkirk
JUNE:
Italy declares war on France and Britain
German troops enter Paris
France signs an armistice with Germany
Italy bombs Malta in the Mediterranean
JULY:
German U-boats inflict heavy losses on Allied convoys in the Atlantic
Britain sends warships to neutralise the French fleet in North Africa
The Battle of Britain begins
SEPTEMBER:
Luftwaffe air raids begin the Blitz – the bombing of London and other British cities
Italian troops advance from Libya into Egypt
Germany, Italy and Japan sign the Tripartite Pact
OCTOBER:
Italy invades Greece; Greek forces, aided by the British, mount a counterattack
DECEMBER:
British troops at Sidi Barrani, Egypt, force the Italians to retreat

1941

JANUARY:
Allied units capture Tobruk in Libya
British forces in Sudan attack Italian East Africa
FEBRUARY:
Allies defeat Italy at Benghazi, Libya
Rommel's Afrika Korps arrive in Tripoli
MARCH:
The Africa Korps drive British troops back from El Agheila
APRIL:
German, Italian and Hungarian units invade Yugoslavia
German forces invade Greece
The Afrika Korps beseige Tobruk
MAY:
The British sink the German battleship *Bismarck*
JUNE:
German troops invade the Soviet Union
JULY:
German forces advance to within 16 kilometres (10 miles) of Kiev
AUGUST:
The United States bans the export of oil to Japan
SEPTEMBER:
German forces start the siege of Leningrad
German Army Group Centre advances on Moscow
NOVEMBER:
British troops begin an attack to relieve Tobruk
The Allies liberate Ethiopia
DECEMBER:
Japanese aircraft attack the U.S. Pacific Fleet at Pearl Harbor
Japan declares war on the United States and Britain
The United States, Britain and the Free French declare war on Japan
Japanese forces invade the Philippines, Malaya and Thailand, and defeat the British garrison in Hong Kong

1942

JANUARY:
Japan attacks the Dutch East Indies and invades Burma
Rommel launches a new offensive in Libya

FEBRUARY:

Singapore surrenders to the Japanese

APRIL:

The Bataan Peninsula in the Philippines falls to the Japanese

MAY:

U.S. and Japanese fleets clash at the Battle of the Coral Sea

Rommel attacks the Gazala Line in Libya

JUNE:

The U.S. Navy defeats the Japanese at the Battle of Midway

Rommel recaptures Tobruk and the Allies retreat to Egypt

JULY:

The Germans take Sebastopol after a long siege and advance into the Caucasus

AUGUST:

U.S. Marines encounter fierce Japanese resistance in the Solomons

SEPTEMBER–OCTOBER:

Allied forces defeat Axis troops at El Alamein, Egypt – the first major Allied victory of the war

NOVEMBER:

U.S. and British troops land in Morocco and Algeria

1943

FEBRUARY:

The German Sixth Army surrenders at Stalingrad

The Japanese evacuate troops from Guadalcanal in the Solomons

MAY:

Axis forces in Tunisia surrender, ending the campaign in North Africa

JULY:

U.S. troops make landings on New Georgia Island in the Solomons

The Red Army wins the Battle of Kursk

Allied troops land on Sicily

British bombers conduct massive raids on Hamburg

AUGUST:

German forces occupy Italy

SEPTEMBER:

Allied units begin landings on mainland Italy

Italy surrenders, prompting a German invasion of northern Italy

OCTOBER:

The Red Army liberates the Caucasus

NOVEMBER:

U.S. carrier aircraft attack Rabaul in the Solomons

1944

JANUARY:

The German siege of Leningrad ends

FEBRUARY:

U.S. forces conquer the Marshall Islands

MARCH:

The Soviet offensive reaches the Dniester River

Allied aircraft bomb the monastery at Monte Cassino in Italy

JUNE:

U.S. troops enter the city of Rome

D-Day–the Allies begin the invasion of northern Europe

U.S. aircraft defeat the Japanese fleet at the Battle of the Philippine Sea

JULY:

The Red Army begins its offensive to clear the Baltic states

Soviet tanks enter Poland

AUGUST:

Japanese troops withdraw from Myitkyina in Burma

French forces liberate Paris

Allied units liberate towns in France, Belgium and the Netherlands

OCTOBER:

Soviet and Yugoslavian troops capture Belgrade, the Yugoslav capital

The Japanese suffer defeat at the Battle of Leyte Gulf

DECEMBER:

Hitler counterattacks in the Ardennes in the Battle of the Bulge

1945

JANUARY:

The U.S. Army lands on Luzon in the Philippines

The Red Army liberates Auschwitz

Most of Poland and Czechoslovakia are liberated by the Allies

FEBRUARY:

U.S. troops take the Philippine capital, Manila

U.S. Marines land on the island of Iwo Jima

Soviet troops strike west across Germany

The U.S. Army heads towards the River Rhine

APRIL:

U.S. troops land on the island of Okinawa

Mussolini is shot by partisans

Soviet troops assault Berlin

Hitler commits suicide in his bunker

MAY:

All active German forces surrender

JUNE:

Japanese resistance ends in Burma and on Okinawa

AUGUST:

Atomic bombs are dropped on Hiroshima and Nagasaki

Japan surrenders

World War II: Europe

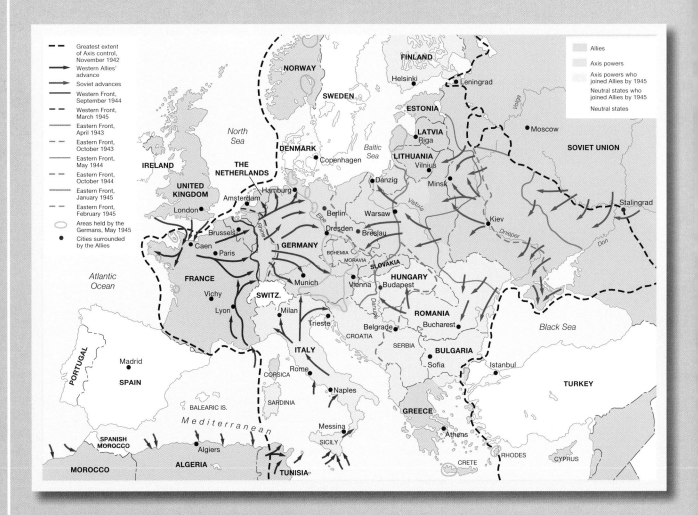

The war began with rapid German advances through the Low Countries and northern France. In June 1941 German armies struck through eastern Europe into the Soviet Union, besieging Leningrad and Stalingrad. However, Allied landings in North Africa led to eventual victory there and opened the way for the invasion of Sicily and then of the Italian peninsula itself, forcing Italy to surrender. In the east the defeat of the German Sixth Army at Stalingrad forced a long retreat during which German forces were harried by communist guerrillas at all moments. In June 1944 Allied forces landed in northern France on D-Day and began to fight their way toward Berlin. As the Soviet advance closed in and the Americans and British crossed the Rhine River into Germany, defeat became inevitable. Hitler committed suicide in his bunker at the heart of his failed Reich, or empire.

World War II: The Pacific

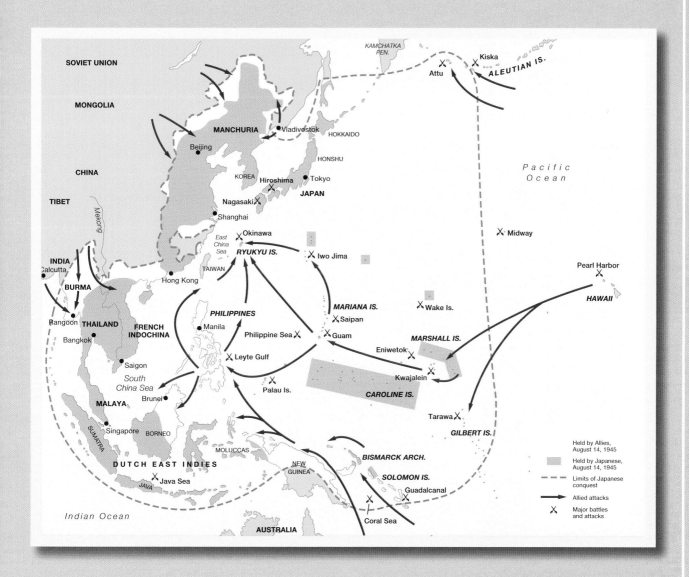

The Pacific conflict began with swift Japanese advances and occupation of territory throughout Southeast Asia, Malaya, the East Indies, the Philippines and the island groups of the Pacific. The U.S. fleet was weakened by the attack on Pearl Harbor, but the damage it suffered was repaired remarkably quickly. After the naval victory at Midway in June 1942, U.S. commanders fought a campaign of 'island hopping', overcoming strong local Japanese resistance to establish a series of stepping stones that would bring their bombers close enough to attack the Japanese home islands. Meanwhile, British and Indian troops pushed back the Japanese advance from Burma.

Biographies

Neville Chamberlain

British statesman. Conservative prime minister from 1937 to 1940, Chamberlain led the policy of appeasement of Hitler. He argued that giving in to Hitler's demands was the best way to prevent war. When the policy failed, he resigned in favour of Winston Churchill.

Churchill, Winston

British statesman. Churchill became British prime minister in May 1940 after a controversial political career. He was an energetic, inspiring and imaginative leader. His powerful speeches and his careful cultivation of Britain's U.S. allies were vital to the Allies' war effort. After the war's end Churchill was defeated in a general election, but he later became prime minister again in 1951.

De Gaulle, Charles

French statesman. French army officer De Gaulle escaped to London after the German invasion of France in 1939 and set up the Free French to oppose the Vichy regime's collaboration with Germany. Under De Gaulle's leadership, the Free French grew to include some 300,000 fighters, including partisans of the French Resistance. In 1945 he was elected president of France and later founded the Fifth Republic.

Eisenhower, Dwight D.

U.S. general. Eisenhower was part of the U.S. war plans division when he was promoted in June 1942 to become commander of U.S. forces in Europe. He led the Allied landings in North Africa and Sicily and the capture of Rome. As supreme commander of Allied forces, he led the D-Day landings in northern France and the liberation of Paris and advance into Germany. His popularity was reflected by his election in 1952 as the 34th president of the United States, a position he held for 12 years.

Goebbels, Joseph

Nazi leader. Joseph Goebbels was the head of Nazi Party propaganda and later became minister of propaganda in the Nazi government. He used mass media and cinema skilfully to promote Nazi views. At the end of the war, he killed his children and committed suicide with his wife.

Hirohito

Emperor of Japan. Hirohito reluctantly approved the growth of army power and the militarization of Japanese society. He also backed the aggressive foreign policy that eventually led to war, but in 1945 he supported the leaders who wanted to surrender unconditionally. After the war he gave up his divine status and became a constitutional monarch.

Hitler, Adolf

Dictator of Germany. After serving as a soldier in World War I, Adolf Hitler joined a minor political party that he renamed the National Socialist Workers' Party (Nazis). Hitler was elected as chancellor of Germany in 1933 and became leader (Führer) in 1934. His policies were based on anti-Semitism and anti-communism, militarism and the aggressive expansion of Germany. His invasion of Poland in September 1939 sparked the outbreak of the war. Hitler's war leadership was erratic and contributed to Germany's eventual defeat; Hitler himself committed suicide in his bunker in Berlin in the last days of the war.

Hope, Bob

U.S. entertainer. Comedian and singer Bob Hope was one of the biggest movie stars at the start of the war. He became famous for his constant tours of U.S. overseas bases to put on shows for service personnel. Having performed similar tours in later wars in Korea, Vietnam and the Persian Gulf, Hope was acknowledged in 1997 by the U.S. Congress as the first 'Honorary Veteran' in U.S. history.

MacArthur, Douglas

U.S. general. A veteran of World War I, MacArthur commanded the defence of the Philippines against Japan in 1941 before becoming supreme Allied commander in the Southwest Pacific. He commanded the U.S. attacks on New Guinea and the Philippines. After the end of the war, he became supreme Allied commander of Japan and oversaw the country's rapid postwar recovery.

Miller, Dorrie

Miller was an African-American seaman who served at Pearl Harbor in December 1941. Although at the time African Americans were only allowed to serve as orderlies, his courage during the Japanese attack earned him the Navy Cross and made him a national hero.

Montgomery, Bernard

British field marshal. Montgomery led the British Eighth Army in North Africa, where it defeated Rommel's Afrika Korps, and then shared joint command of the invasion of Sicily and Italy. He collaborated with U.S. general Eisenhower on planning the D-Day landings in France, where he commanded all land forces; Montgomery went on to command an army group in the advance toward Germany, where he eventually received the German surrender.

Mussolini, Benito

Italian dictator. Mussolini came to power in Italy in 1922 promoting fascism, a political philosophy based on a militaristic form of nationalism. He led attempts to re-create an Italian empire with overseas conquests. Mussolini became Hitler's ally in 1936 and entered the war on the Nazis' side. Italian campaigns went badly in the Balkans and North Africa, however. When the Allies invaded Italy in 1943 Mussolini was sacked by the king; he became president of a puppet German republic in northern Italy. He was executed by Italian partisan fighters at the end of the war.

Rommel, Erwin

German field marshal. Rommel was a tank commander who led the Afrika Korps in North Africa and later led the defence of northern France against the Allied invasion. When he was discovered to be part of a plot to assassinate Adolf Hitler, he was forced to commit suicide.

Roosevelt, Franklin D.

U.S. president. Democrat politician Franklin Delano Roosevelt enjoyed a privileged upbringing before entering politics and becoming governor of New York. He first came to power as president in 1932, when he was elected to apply his New Deal to solve the worst problems of the Great Depression. Reelected in 1936 and again in 1940 he fully supported the Allies, offering supplies to help fight the Germans. He was reelected in 1944, the only president to be elected for four terms, but died in office shortly before the end of the war against Japan.

Rosie the Riveter

A fictional American worker who first appeared in a popular song but whose image then appeared on posters and stamps to encourage women to take industrial jobs during the war. The various depictions of Rosie were based on a number of specific individual workers.

Stalin, Joseph

Soviet dictator. Stalin was a Bolshevik from Georgia who rose to prominence for his skill as an administrator. In 1922 he became general secretary of the Communist Party of the Soviet Union founded by Lenin. Stalin introduced programs to encourage agriculture and industry and in the 1930s got rid of many thousands of potential enemies in purges, having them jailed or executed. Having made a pact with Hitler in 1939, he was surprised when Hitler invaded the Soviet Union in 1941 but rallied the Red Army to eventual victory. At the end of the war, he imposed Soviet rule on eastern Europe.

Yamamoto, Isoroko

Japanese admiral. Yamamoto was a visionary naval planner who planned Japan's attack on the U.S. base at Pearl Harbor and its early Pacific campaigns. He was killed when the Americans shot down his aircraft in 1943, alerted by decoded Japanese radio communications.

Glossary

Allies One of the two groups of combatants in the war. The main Allies were Britain, the Soviet Union, the United States, British Empire troops, and free forces from occupied nations.

antibiotic A medicine that can halt the spread of infection.

anti-Semitism A hatred of Jews and Judaism.

armistice A temporary halt in fighting agreed to by both sides.

armour A term referring to armoured vehicles, such as tanks.

artillery Large weapons such as big guns and howitzers.

Aryan In Nazi propaganda, relating to a mythical master race of Nordic peoples.

Axis One of the two groups of combatants in the war. The leading Axis powers were Germany, Italy, and Japan.

blitzkrieg A German word meaning "lightning war." It referred to the tactic of rapid land advance supported by great airpower.

Bolsheviks Members of the Communist Party that took power in Russia after the 1917 Revolution.

casualty Someone who is killed or wounded in conflict, or who is missing but probably dead.

collaborator Someone who works with members of enemy forces who are occupying his or her country.

communism A political philosophy based on state control of the economy and distribution of wealth, followed in the Soviet Union from 1917 and in China from 1948.

corps A military formation smaller than an army, made up of a number of divisions operating together under a general.

counteroffensive A set of attacks that defend against enemy attacks.

empire A number of countries governed by a single country.

embargo An order to temporarily stop something, especially trading.

espionage The use of spies or secret agents to obtain information about the plans of a foreign government.

evacuation The act of moving someone from danger to a safe position.

Fascism A political philosophy promoted by Mussolini in Italy based on dictatorial leadership, nationalism and the importance of the state over the individual.

garrison A group of troops placed to defend a location.

Holocaust The systematic German campaign to exterminate millions of Jews and others.

hygiene Following practices, such as keeping clean, that support the maintenance of good health.

independence The state of self-government for a people or nation.

infantry Soldiers who are trained to fight on foot, or in vehicles.

kamikaze Japanese for "divine wind"; the name refers to Japan's suicide pilots.

landing craft Shallow-bottomed boats designed to carry troops and supplies from ships to the shore.

Marine A soldier who serves in close association with naval forces.

materiel A word that describes all the equipment and supplies used by military forces.

morale A sense of common purpose and positive spirits among a group of people or a whole population

occupation The seizure and control of an area by military force.

offensive A planned military attack.

patriotism A love for and promotion of one's country.

propaganda Material such as images, broadcasts or writings that aims to influence the ideas or behaviour of a group of people.

rationing A system of limiting food and other supplies to ensure that everyone gets a similar amount.

reconnaissance A small-scale survey of enemy territory to gather information.

resources Natural materials that are the basis of economic wealth, such as oil, rubber, and agricultural produce.

strategy A detailed plan for achieving success.

strongpoint Any defensive position that has been strengthened to withstand an attack.

siege A military blockade of a place, such as a city, to force it to surrender.

taxes Fees on earnings or financial transactions used by governments to raise money from their citizens.

troops Groups of soldiers.

war bonds A form of investment used by governments in wartime to raise money from savers.

Further Reading

Books

Adams, Simon. *Occupation and Resistance* (Documenting World War II). Wayland, 2008.

Black, Hermann. *World War II, 1939–1945* (Wars Day-by-Day). Brown Bear Reference, 2008.

The Blitz. World War II Replica Memorabilia Pack. Resources for Teaching, 2010.

Burgan, Michael. *America in World War II* (Wars That Changed American History). World Almanac Library, 2006.

Cross, Vince. *Blitz: a Wartime Girl's Diary, 1940–1941* (My Story). Scholastic, 2008.

Deary, Terry, and Mike Phillips. *The Blitz* (Horrible Histories Handbooks). Scholastic 2009.

Dowswell, Paul. *Usborne Introduction to the Second World War.* Usborne Publishing Ltd., 2005.

Gardiner, Juliet. *The Children's War: The Second World War Through the Eyes of the Children of Britain.* Portrait, 2005.

Heppelwhite, Peter. *An Evacuee's Journey* (History Journeys). Wayland, 2004.

Hosch, William L. *World War II: People, Politics and Power* (America at War). Rosen Education Service, 2009.

MacDonald, Fiona. *World War II: Life on the Home Front: A Primary Source History* (In Their Own Words). Gareth Stevens Publishing, 2009.

McNeese, Tim. *World War II: 1939–1945* (Discovering U.S. History). Chelsea House Publishers, 2010.

O'Shei, Tim. *World War II Spies.* Edge Books, 2008.

Price, Sean. *Rosie the Riveter: Women in World War II.* Raintree, 2008.

Price, Sean. *The Art of War: The Posters of World War II* (American History Through Primary Sources). Raintree, 2008.

Ross, Stuart. *The Blitz* (At Home in World War II). Evans Brothers, 2007.

Ross, Stuart. *Evacuation* (At Home in World War II). Evans Brothers, 2007.

Ross, Stuart. *Rationing* (At Home in World War II). Evans Brothers, 2007.

Tonge, Neil. *The Rise of the Nazis* (Documentary World War II). Wayland, 2008.

Wagner, Melissa, and Dan Bryant. *The Big Book of World War II: Fascinating Facts about World War II Including Maps, Historic Photographs and Timelines.* Perseus Books, 2009.

World War II (10 volumes). Grolier Educational, 2006.

World War II (Eyewitness). Dorling Kindersley, 2007.

Websites

www.bbc.co.uk/history/worldwars/wwtwo/
Causes, events and people of the war.

http://www.bbc.co.uk/schools/primaryhistory/world_war2/
Interactive information on what it was like to be a child during the war.

http://www.spartacus.schoolnet.co.uk/2WW.htm
Spartacus Education site on the war.

http://www.nationalarchives.gov.uk/education/worldwar2/
U.S. National Archives primary sources on the war.

http://www.historylearningsite.co.uk/WORLD%20WAR%20TWO.htm
History Learning Site guide to the war.

http://www.telegraph.co.uk/news/newstopics/world-war-2/
Daily Telegraph archive of articles from wartime and from the 70th anniversary of its outbreak.

www.war-experience.org
The Second World War Experience Centre.

www.ibiblio.org/pha
A collection of primary World War II source materials.

www.worldwar-2.net
Complete World War II day-by-day timeline.

http://www.iwm.org.uk/searchlight/server.php?change=SearchlightGalleryView&changeNav=home
Imperial War Museum, London, guide to collections.

Index